# Which Really Came First: Creation or Evolution?

by

William B. C. Parnell

Palm Coast FL 32164

Which Really Came First: Creation or Evolution?

By William B. C. Parnell

© 2012 by William B.C. Parnell   All Rights Reserved.

ISBN: 978-1-935795-77-3

Out of Your Mind Publishing LLC
PO Box 353431
Palm Coast, FL 32135-3431
www.outofyourmindpublishing.com

All Rights Reserved. No part of this book may be reproduced stored in a retrieval system, or transmitted, in any form or by any means, electronic, mechanical, photocopying, recording, or otherwise, without permission in writing from Out of Your Mind Publishing LLC.

Front Cover Design by Cindy Grudo, Out of Your Mind Publishing LLC

Back Cover Coat of Arms by William B.C. Parnell

All rights reserved

Printed in the United States of America

## Table of Contents

Introduction

Chapter One: Religion ..................................................................1

Chapter Two: Evolution................................................................7

Chapter Three: Universal Force ................................................. 11

Chapter Four: God Revealed...................................................... 13

Chapter Five: Free Will............................................................... 17

Chapter Six: Reincarnation......................................................... 19

Chapter Seven: Which Came First? ........................................... 21

Chapter Eight: Summary ............................................................ 23

# INTRODUCTION

Creation or Evolution:

Which theory correctly explains our existence and the existence of the universe? Does one exclude the other? Are there truths to be learned from both?

This writing attempts to put both in perspective with each other and offers a possible answer as to which actually came first. It also delves into what influences each have had on each other

# CHAPTER ONE: RELIGION

According to the Jewish Torah and the Christian Bible Testimony, a 'God' created "heaven and earth"; including all of the existence in six days, literally speaking. Most experts of faith accept this view, fully understanding how long in modern time measurement of a day was in the act of creation. We now accept a day as one rotation of the earth around the sun, when during creation a day could have meant thousands of years, but expressed as a day in time.

Humans have interpreted biblical text in many different ways. The Bible was not written when events happened, but after those events occurred, often by many centuries. Stories were passed down from generation to generation by word of mouth through stories before they were written down.

Thus past history was flavored by individual thoughts and interpretations. Modern man embraces the interpretation he is most satisfied with and can understand best. And so the different faiths have developed.

Indeed today differences of opinions have resulted in the many divisional sects of faith. Witness the variations in practices of Judaism, Christianity, Buddhism, and Islam. Each professes to be the only true faith and their rituals to be the true methods of prayer and salvation.

What is certain is that all modern faith and sects agree that there is only on true 'God' and that 'He' or 'She' exists in 'heaven' beyond earth and man.

Webster's dictionary defines heaven as "1.) The expanse of space that

seems to be over the earth like a dome; 2.) The dwelling place of the Deity; 3.) The joyful abode of the blessed dead; 4.) Heaven is 'God.'"

Let us look at the story of creation. "From the dark emptiness of space, God created the earth and heavens, then light and separated the light from darkness. This the first day."

"God called the earth below *the firmament* to come together to form dry land. The land was called earth, and the waters called sea. This was the second day."

"On the dry land God created grasses, trees, and fruit; each with their particular seeds for procreation in like kind. This was the third day."

"God created stars in the heavens or darkness of space; stars as we know as suns, moons, galaxies. This is the fourth day."

"God created life in the seas and in the air." (Life in this meaning is most living microorganisms of various forms. This started evolution to fish and birds.) This was the fifth day."

"God created living creatures on the earth after his own kind." Some believe he is in a bodily form as man is today; but this could be interpreted as "after, or like, his splendid form. i.e. the soul of God." "He created man from the earth and women from the rib of man. This is the sixth day."

Throughout all of recorded history, gods have been portrayed as larger than life and as greater than man. We have always referred to objects as living or inanimate, as masculine or feminine, so too has God been referred to as 'He' or 'She'. Ancient civilizations created pantheons of gods with separate and

distinct powers or areas of influences. In all references, a god is all knowing, everlasting, all powerful, and infallible; that presides over all beings; one that is both revengeful and forgiving; one that exists but cannot be seen. Modern man holds all these attributes to be true of the "God we know."

All agree, also, that we see God working in our lives and in nature, giving us proof enough of His existence.

---

All biblical references from:
The Holy Bible (containing the Old and New Testaments)
King James Version Set Forth in 1611

American Bible Society
Instituted in the Year 1816
New York

# CHAPTER TWO: EVOLUTION

Webster's dictionary defines evolution as a "process to which the whole universe is a progression of interrelated phenomena; the gradual and relatively peaceful set of prescribed movements."

Promoters of the evolution theory base creation's beginning with a soup of elements interacting and merging to form all material and life forms over an exceptionally long period of time, as measured by carbon dating. Most exponents of pure science hold this the truth of creation: starting with the random convergence of various elements in the void of space, resulting in the planets, galaxies, suns, earth, and the Milky Way. This could explain why planets are composed of various elements of iron, ice, rocks, and gases.

This would imply that all elements of life, as well, resulted in the accidental random convergence of elements like atoms, genes, DNA, oxygen, nitrogen, water, carbon, sulfur, and amino acids.

Science traces evolution of life thru the changes in the earth's formation. From the development of life in the sea: amoebas to one cell beings, to multiple cell animals, to fish, to walking land animals, to winged birds, to Cro-Magnon man, to Homo sapiens.

All evolution, per science, has been by random interaction and circumstances of habitat, environment, propagation, and in the geographical changes in the earth.

Today we can see the results of these changes in the differences in the human races, due to extremes in the habitat and interbreeding. The same is true among lower animals, even the pollination of plants in nature and the lab.

By natural action or by man's intervention, the earth is constantly changing or evolving (i.e., earthquakes, tectonic shifts, hurricanes, earth warming, changing in the flow of the jet stream, and the tilting of the earth's axis).

Man has also changed or evolved their generation by increased height, strength, endurance, resistance to diseases, and increased mental development. Man by nature is a curious animal; one who seeks new knowledge and enjoys problem solving (i.e. mathematics, space travel, medical advances, and genetic research). I believe there is no limit to man's development.

# CHAPTER THREE: UNIVERSAL FORCE

I champion the theory that God exists in spiritual form; a form of pure energy.

Perhaps God did not create man in his physical form, but in his spiritual form, and that he exists as a soul in man. I believe God to be a universal and all incumbent soul. When conception takes place, God imparts a spark of that soul to start life, whether in man or nature, but indeed in all living existence.

The ancient Druids and modern naturists attribute a spirit (or soul) in all living plants and animal life.

In this writing I conform to the humanization of the "universal force" as "God." I accept Jesus as the extension of his soul, to walk upon the earth as a physical form; developing and growing into manhood, to be an example and teacher; a witness to the existence of one true God.

Consider the universal force to be like a container of water. When conception occurs, "the spark" or say a drop of water from that container or "soul" conceives a life. Since there is always a balance in all things, would the balance be tilted with the creation of an increasing number of souls?

Like clouds that absorb water from the oceans by evaporation, this universal soul absolves all the souls or droplets of water that are lost in wars, natural disasters, accidents, and naturally expired life. Thus, a balance in the universal force is maintained.

After all major wars, or catastrophes, the world population increases. The wonder is that the container expands, more than before; and so to the never ending soul of God.

# CHAPTER FOUR: GOD REVEALED

How could God make himself known to man? Only by actions and casual effects that are beyond man's capability to reproduce. The universal force, "God," proves himself in causing natural effects in nature and in the interaction thru events in man's personal lives.

God makes himself known to man by offering a spark of life to create a child, Jesus, who grew, developed and experienced all the physical life that man experiences. How better to communicate with man than to walk with man as a physical being. One that has within, the power and nature of universal force. How else could a physical man perform the miracles attributed to him in historical writing?

In this physical form, God lived among man, leading and teaching man how to use the talents he has been given, and how to fit into all of creation.

A primary teaching was about free will, and the choices of good or bad, and the consequences that result. All faiths offer the same teaching.

To prove the power and nature of God, he called upon his physical form on earth to satisfy prophecies revealed. He offered himself to be sacrificed to erase the misguided choices of early man. The spark of life, the universal soul of his physical self was withdrawn, causing the experience of death, as earthly man would experience. Life was restored in three days to demonstrate the power of the force. Accounts exist of man's witnessing the spiritual soul ascending to return to God's domain.

Science does not have the power to create or maintain the working of nature or the universe. Science has, however, helped to create life by the joining of an egg and sperm in a test tube, but the spark of life or that spark of soul, still comes from God. God also reveals himself through answering of prayers. Prayers by individuals and by mass groups have resulted in terminal life being healed through seemingly miraculous acts of an intervening force.

# CHAPTER FIVE: FREE WILL

To understand diversity of faiths, one must understand free will. Man is created with the gift of free will, or the ability to independently choose fewer options of thoughts and actions. Choosing between actions that are either advantageous or detrimental to one's individual well being.

Free will in animals tends to a natural selection of the species, or the selection of the fittest and strongest for procreation of the species. Free will in lower animals has however resulted in new species; i.e. the mule.

The same is true of man's free will that takes extreme paths. One may choose to be homogeneous; loving of one another's well being, cooperative and in support of the species, and understanding of his faith's interpretation of life. Others may choose to be indulgent, greedy, self centered, and non-caring of others; even harmful to the extreme against humanity. All agree these are the opposite paths of good and evil; each choice has rewards or consequences as judged by groups of social norms.

Free will in man has also led to mixed species, or mixed races; that is, mixed genes. Throughout history many have survived and established separate, flourishing cultures of their own. An example is the mixing of Cro-Magnon man and Homo sapiens.

Existing in historical record is free will resulting in homosexual lifestyles among the centuries. These lifestyles have done nothing to enhance man's ultimate and innate biological desire for procreation of the species.

# CHAPTER SIX: REINCARNATION

Reincarnation is a belief theory that rebirth of the soul can occur from a living entity into a new entity. A lower entity, like an insect or an animal would or could be reform into a higher entity in the evolutionary chain. Also, the learned experiences, instincts, and memories of that last existence are transferred into the next.

Could the soul of a past thinking person be reincarnated into a newly conceived human, with all the knowledge and skill of the past soul intact?

This could explain how human prodigies are formed: being from early years, exhibiting extraordinary abilities in mathematics, music, art, science, language, and problem solving. Abilities far beyond their physical age or education.

Does reincarnation follow the same step by step progression as did the creation of the universe and man? Would this in time result in all humans having greater and greater possession of unlimited knowledge and skills? Perhaps.

With better nutrition and control of disease, man has already exhibited general increase in height, size, and strength over older generations; even longer lives.

The Hindu caste system of India proposes that living beings born into a certain caste are reborn into another caste over and over again, depending on faith and devotion until "Nirvana" or peace is achieved.

# CHAPTER SEVEN: WHICH CAME FIRST?

It may become clear that this writer believes, without a doubt, that a universal force or energy was the guiding force in the creation of all that we know. Evolution then has been a result of action after action, cause or effect, accidental or purposeful of previous actions. There had to be an order in the chaos of space, guiding the step by step progression of events leading to the universe we know today; and that guiding force was God, the universal force of creation.

# CHAPTER EIGHT: SUMMARY

In summary, this writer submits the following conclusion for the reader's consideration and debate.

The vastness of space, though void of light, is not a vast ocean of nothingness, but contains all the elements of all existence. In that expanse is a force that collected and molded those various elements into what we know and understand as the cosmos. An attempt to understand that process is explained by faith and the existence of God. Science begins its explanation with the already existing physical evidence of earth and celestial bodies in space.

Faith explains creation without physical proof. The existence of creation is proof enough as well as faith, or belief in God, who started order from nothingness and who established the laws of nature, and the law of cause and effect into motion. These are the very effects that evolution calls upon as proof of its theory.

Indeed cause and effect in the cosmos can be witnesses in the interaction of the stellar bodies with the earth, as disasters or fruitful times.

Therefore, a 'God' known by many names exists in the form of a universal force, not a physical form. Skeptics may question the hypothesis of a universal force by asking how it came into existence.

I contend that the universal force IS the cosmos and is energized by perpetual motion. The closest man can achieve perpetual motion is the Gyro; however, it will slow down and stop due to friction. I suspect the continuous motion of elements in the cosmos generates the perpetual static energy that fuels and maintains the universal force.

William B. C. Parnell, a native Tennessean, graduated from Murphy High school in Mobile, Alabama and earned a Bachelor of Science degree from Troy University in Alabama, with minors in Art and Education.

He is a veteran of the Korean War, with an honorable discharge. He is currently retired from the U.S. Coast Guard and resides in Palm Coast, Florida.

Interest in history and a study of comparative religions prompted the writing of this publication.

www.ingramcontent.com/pod-product-compliance
Lightning Source LLC
Chambersburg PA
CBHW051431070526
44584CB00023B/3672